THE ANTIGONE POEMS

THE ANTIGONE POEMS

Poems by Marie Slaight
Drawings by Terrence Tasker

An Altaire Publication

National Library of Australia
Cataloguing-in-Publication entry
Author: Slaight, Marie, 1954-
Title: The Antigone Poems / poetry by Marie Slaight; drawings by Terrence Tasker.
Edition: First edition
ISBN: 9780980644708 (Paperback)
Subjects: Sophocles--Influence.
Poetry.
Antigone (Greek mythology) in literature.
Greek drama (Tragedy)
Oedipus (Greek mythology) in literature
Other Authors/Contributors: Tasker, Terrence, 1947-1992, artist.
Dewey Number: A821.4

Printed and bound in Australia
Printed on Stephen Swiss White by Spicers Paper, Australian made
Typeset in Bembo and Goudy Trajan
Book design by Marie Slaight
Cover art by Terrence Tasker

Altaire Productions and Publications
11/1 Greenknowe Avenue
Potts Point, NSW 2011
Australia
www.altaireproductions.com

And sing
My bitter praises
To nails
And flint
And flesh…

CHAPTER ONE

In my skull (all)
The hungry cawing.
Fire
In tormented call.

In my heart (only)
The last flutter.
Anguish
In whispered song.

The sun's flames
Flicker teasingly within
Mocking
All which lies inert.

(Probing, provocative tongues,
They dare death with their insouciance.)

All is aflame with life desirous
And death submits
To the laughing wilds.

Pain increases, suffocation
Then

Like scattered dynamite
Dissembled power
Shattered glass.

Playing on earth
The angel descends to be commanded.
From death to creation
The fire both destroys and creates.

The daemon
The essence
The disorder
I hold sacred.

Rising black...
Scarlet airs
Begging laughter.

When I am used
Then
The innate language.

Potency.
The potency is shattering.
Only the night
Holds jasmine.
Where is my tongue?

If this perfume doesn't burst
It will twist into venom.

The gold is the laughter.
Hysteria
Culminating

Hysteria
The tension preceding
The imminence of explosion
The height of frustration
Then

Chaos consecrates
As all elements find final focus in the erotic...

(The passion comes angrily- danger to damn it- I go to the sun and come back with sweat- wildness gone, fallen ahead- won't be life until the coming heat- movement begins, rocking intensifies- throb overtakes all for fleeing, abandon- the nomadic sense is opening- it is within my power, to draw blood and give it- so much pain- lying ahead in the heat core- the sun's heat, intuitive- intensified firesense- words sparking from hot entrails- time for the hottest bloodflow- then the awakening of all senses, nerves- open, alive, tingling...

I only want to purge of godawful pain- so close to losing me- he has to grip- he's so- what- movement is stronger, hotter, my entire body- where's the sun- where is he- he's not afraid, he knows, he penetrates, he's a fool- to leave me alone – heat's stronger, I'm pulsing- waves of pain, pleasure- I'm his, what of it- thank god- it's time- I can't grow until he returns- sunlove- again, where is he- I wish he would burn- my only love today was the sun- I was in love when the sun took me- now it's gone- I'm cold...

I feel betrayed- by what- no words- I only try so as to fill the gap- whirling's fast, stronger now- I need someone to hold me- so I can hold it- my hurting proves nothing, only that he has the power to pain- I don't give a damn- too much, all wrong, foolish, false- jesus- where is courage- I need it- eagles flying- no one will ever know- I don't want it, can't hold it- closer- to abandon- to core- I want home...)

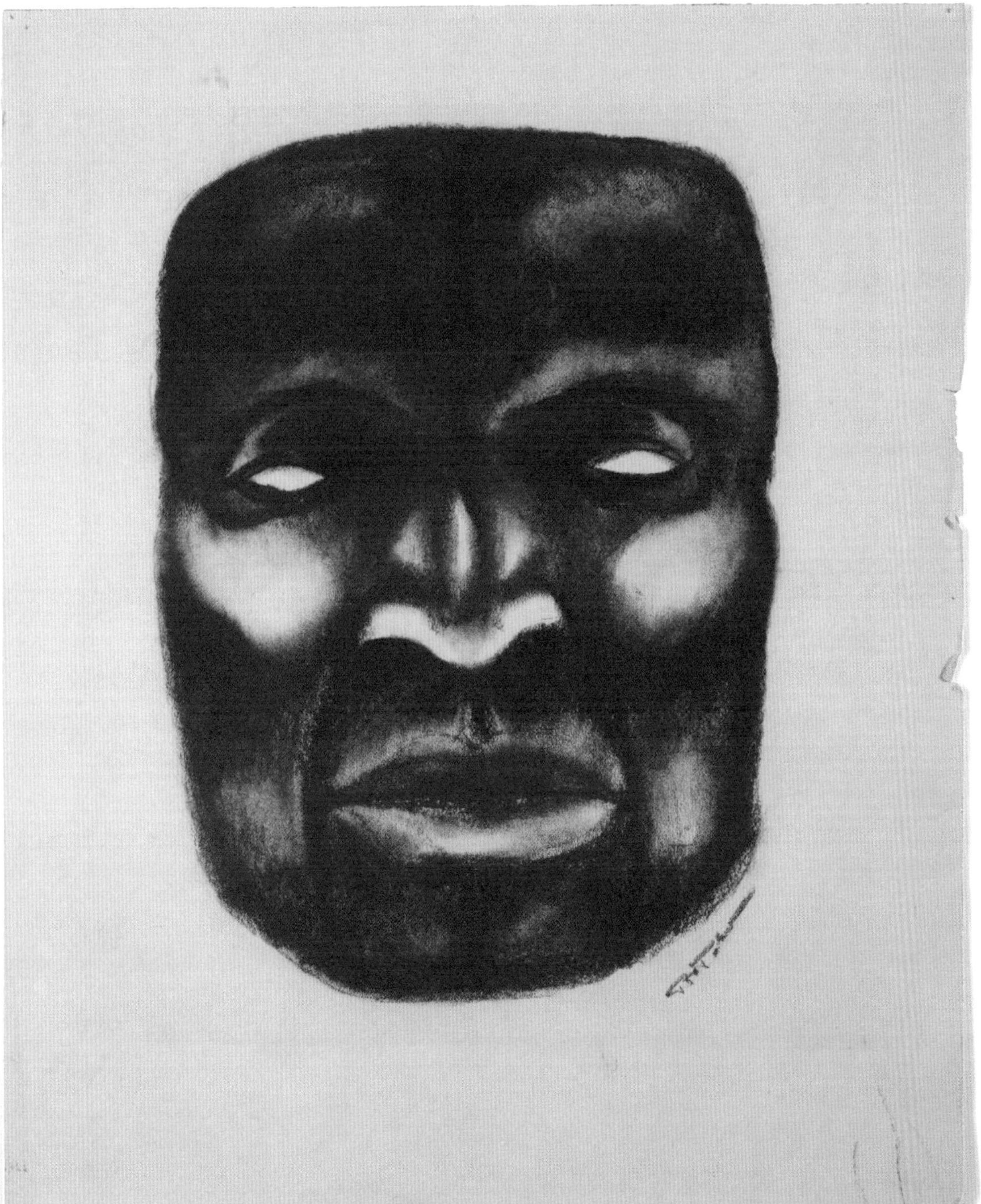

CHAPTER TWO

Daughter of a dark sun
My loins moving
Sweep scarlet over dawn

My peak carrying
Ice-frenzy to the fire
Where ecstasy balms

My lips of pain

Gypsy shackle sacred.
Wrists bound in blood.
Chains
Burnt in anguish
Of daemon ancestry.

Lay stake to my fire.
You tear pain. I cry.

Take whip to my wilds.
You lash fear. I burn.

Carve nails to my flesh.
You draw blood. I drown.

Laughter.
And the violence of gods.

All love pains
Are an aged protest
Wanting fresh surge;
Decrying the ancient throb
Of memories.

Fought order, limits, time.
Time of surrender or death.
To go where no one has been,
The past destroyed by heat.

A fervour
Overtaking
All abysses

Pouring
Ether
In every crevice.

We live our lives
The instant between life and death.
To touch death always,
That is the sun.

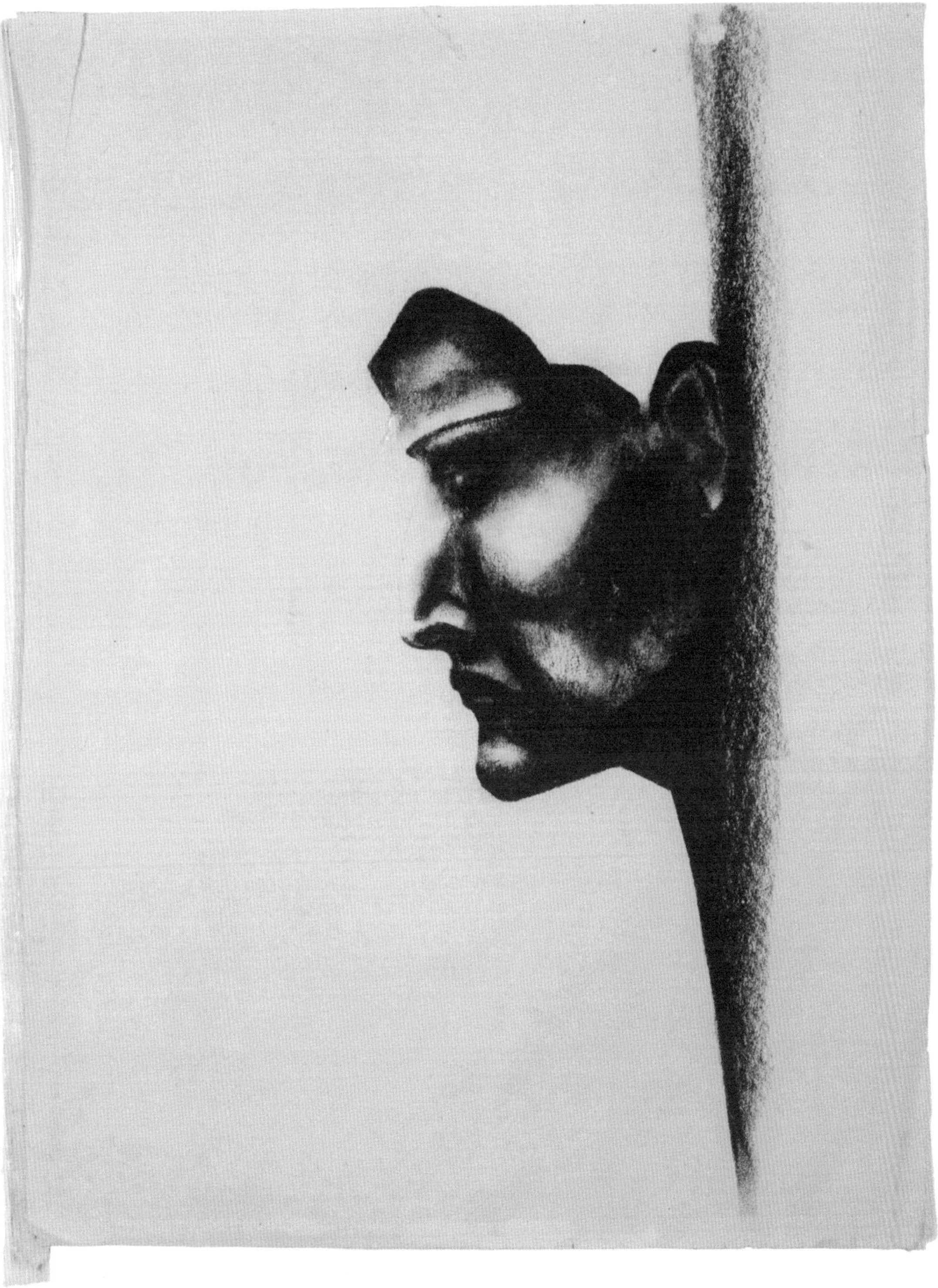

CHAPTER THREE

Loneliness.
Gut in an ache.

No joy.
No pain.

Only the blackened thrust.

Black.
A knives sorrow.

In my heart.
At the twist.

My blood's life.

Black.

THE ANTIGONE POEMS

...And this the earth's secret
Tied dark

Oh lord of the ancient sun

Your daemon is raging
Its fire, my domain...

Bowels break
Blood breaks
Earth cursed
To hungergods.

In this grey dawn
Only
The debauched loneliness
Of your thigh
Flung
Across mine.

Black blossom
Sweeps
Realm of desert ash.

Carver

Twist
Your mark
In flesh.

Sculptor

Smash
This stone
In death.

Your anguish sought this blackened veil.
Your anger wrought this iron hell.

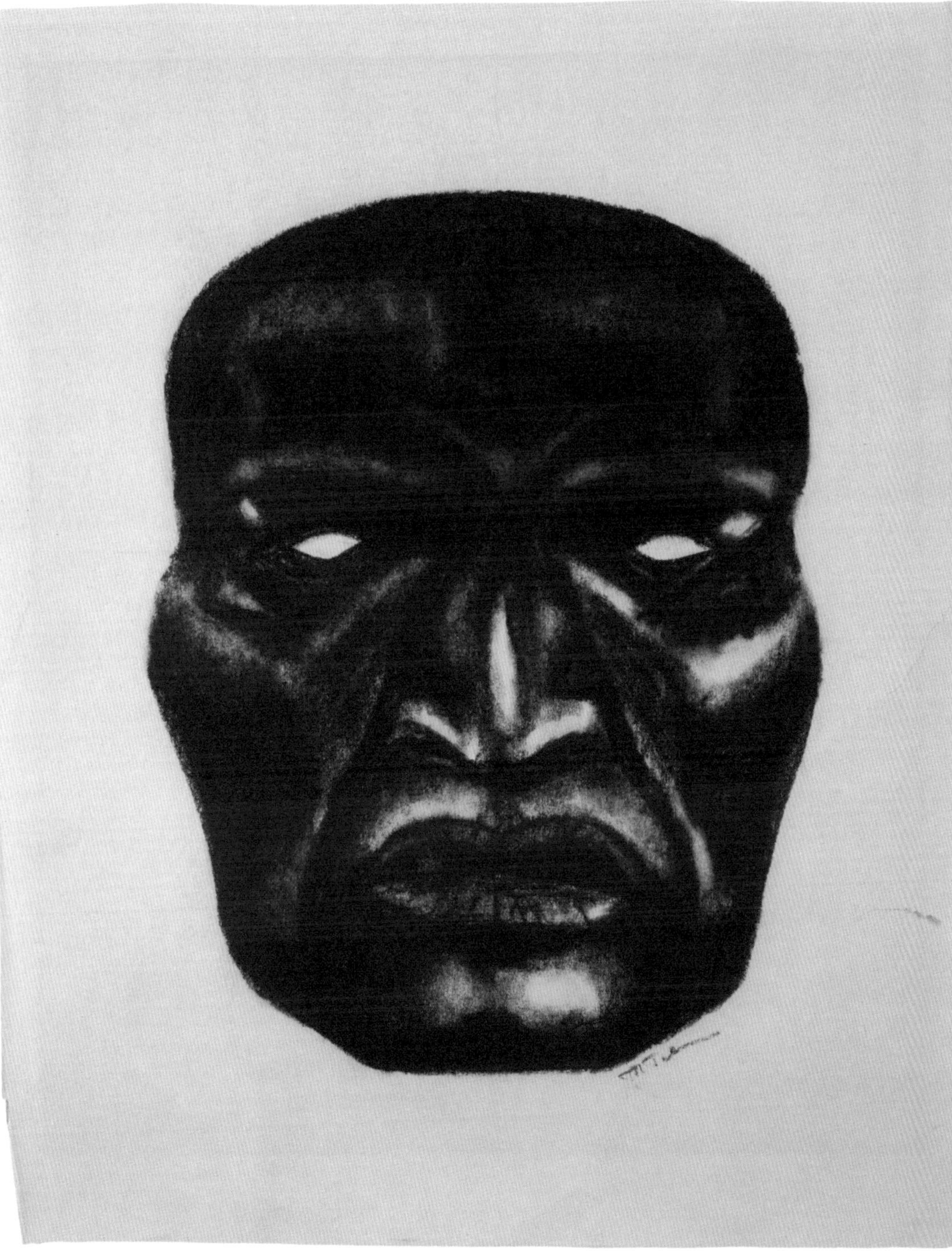

CHAPTER FOUR

This voice
Is afraid to speak.

Afraid
Of the brutal metal
Of its words.

Words that scrape.
Words that scar.
Words that have no peace.

If I utter this voice
This great
Aching scream

Its horror will echo forever.

The empty breast.

A lament
For the lost sweetness

Or a battleground
For the warring dead?

In exile

I walk on blood
I carve a vein
I bear sons

In exile

I carry screams
I seek revenge
I await my return

In exile.

Earth in torment
Earth in tears

Tired

Wracked

Groaning with effort
To remain.

And are we corpses clutching?
(The gnawed bone,
The splintered throat.)

Find my earth.
Reclaim my desire.

...gods speak to the wind and winds whip through me...

I remember only the rage
Screaming
My head breaking
Wanting to kill
You are a murderer
Then nothing.

Silence and decline

And a veil of grey descending.

THE ANTIGONE POEMS

A sword on slate
Impaled
By sunlight.

All is diffusion.

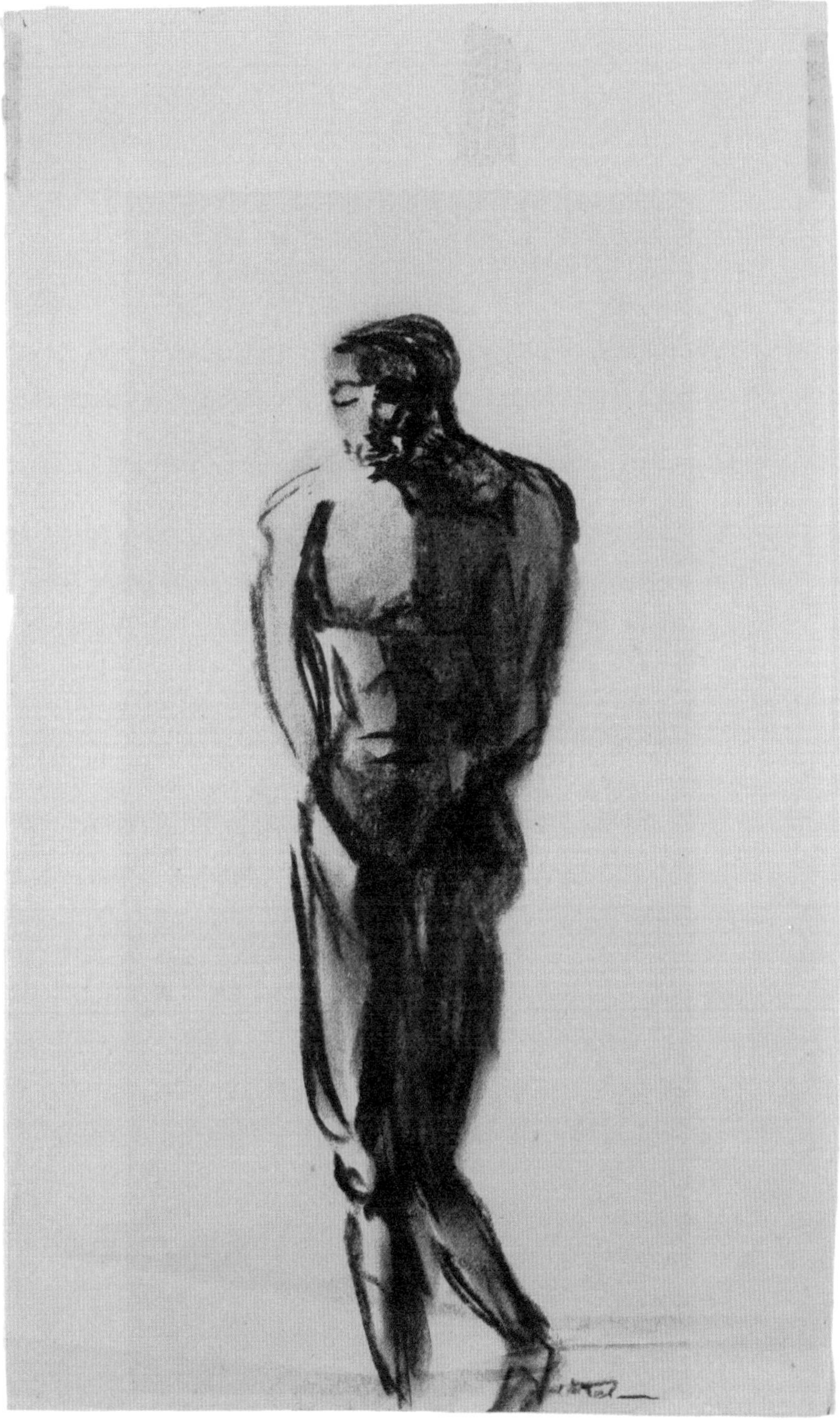

CHAPTER FIVE

Sear
To the sliver
Of membrane

The wound
Aches
To be released.

(Black sun. Green wind.)

Into the angry wilds.

Slice. A razor.
Slice the fatty flesh.

Let blood pour fountains.

No words.
Only the gaping, silent scream.

Go inside
Until one word
Is blood. Until then

Silence.

(Cauterized.)

Let the silence reverberate.
Let the silence break this wall.

The word.

A moan of blood.
Or a spasm.

And is the enslavement
An ode to a greater liberation
Or is it a dead rat in my hand?

There were horrors...

Houses and gutters of curdled blood
Children in chambers

The corpse in the closet
Sitting on trial
And the verdict...

Is it my innocence?

I can't face the dirt
The defilement
Without this dream of barbaric
Lust and grandeur...oh lord of the ancient sun
                                        Your daemon is raging
                                        Its fire, my domain...
And this lord and I
We fight
Over every dollar spent
With the revulsion
Of displaced and dying aristocracy.

And why.

I wanted everything.

To live all lives, all deaths, encompass all women.

To smash every confine.

And what have I done.

I don't know.

I have written a few words

Created a few images

Influenced a few lives.

I live at the corner of St. Lawrence and Pine.

I have three children.

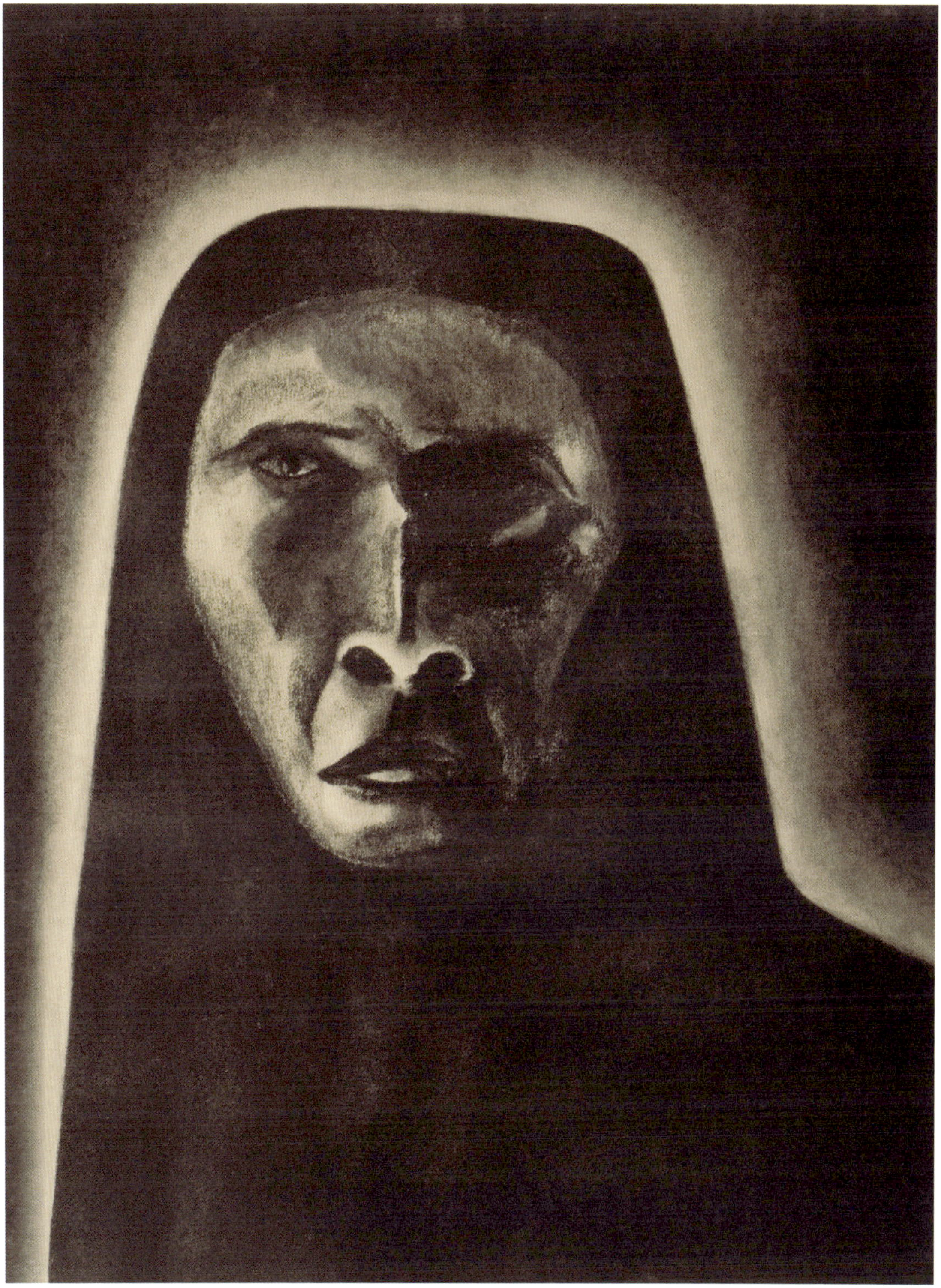

Dedicated to Terrence Tasker
1947 - 1992

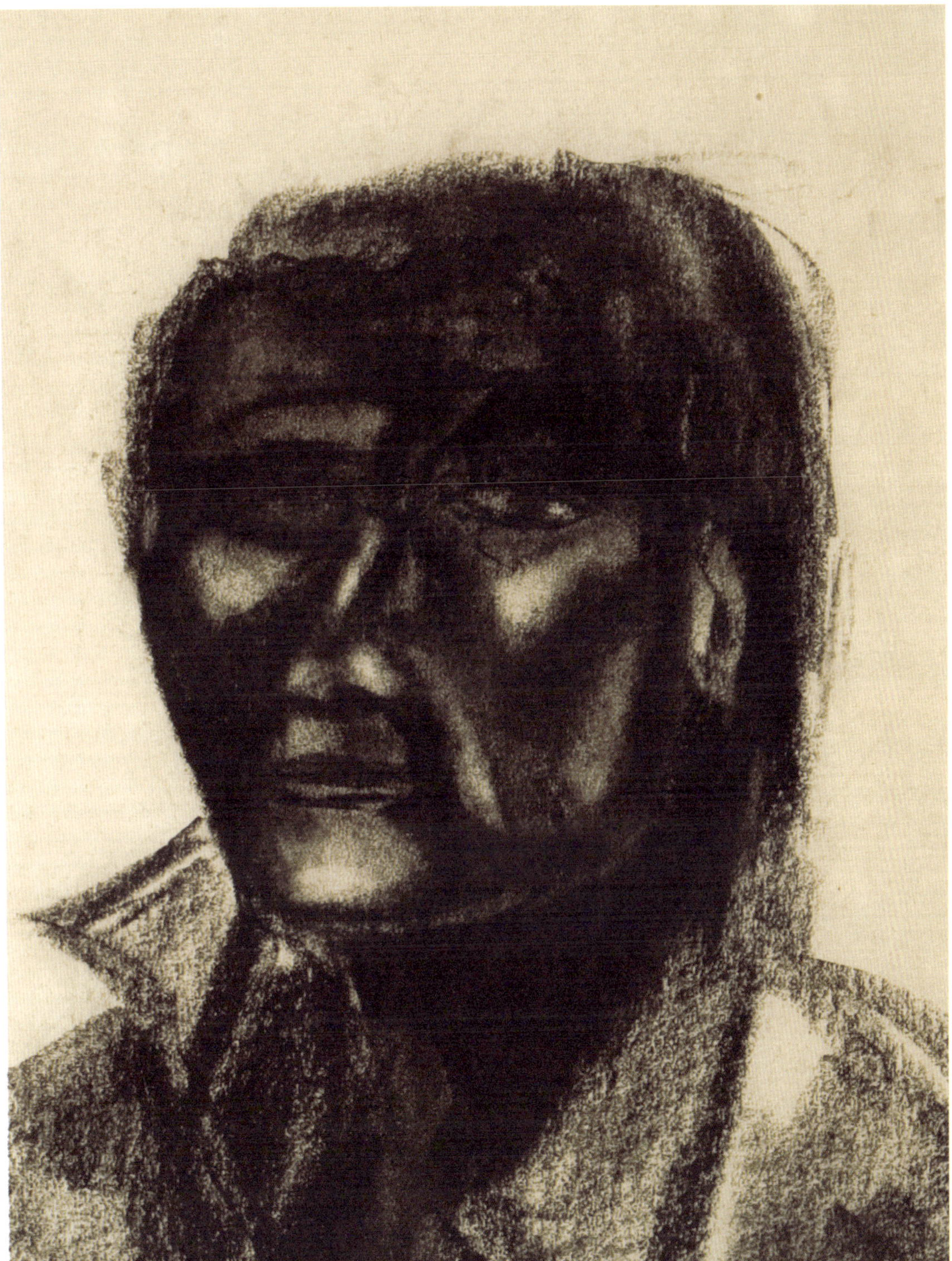

Acknowledgements

George Cotsopoulos
Michael Dascal
Lisa Delfino
Vladan Doslic
Jane Draiman
Jean Napolier
Eli Rill
The Trojan Horse, Toronto circa 1970s
Nikos Tsingos
and
Michael Caleb Tasker

A special thank you to
Allan Slaight